Daze and Knights of Comedic Destruction

Short Tales Illustrating Why the Pun is Mightier Than the "Sword Of"

by Ryan Hargraves

Illustrated by Megan Nolton

Foreword

● ● ● ●

The daze of comedic destruction is a pun, us, and already, I have digressed.

Perhaps you'd like a bit of humor at the beginning of (or at any other point during) your day. Maybe you'd like to allow yourself a couple of hours to enjoy a fun and mind-stimulating journey. Do you find fun in pun and perhaps might enjoy a few puns on the run? If you answered yes to one or more of these statements, then this work is for you! *Daze and Knights* was written to exercise the brain in an entertaining way and will allow you to get to know quite a few interesting fictional characters. Follow them as they experience both harmony and lighthearted discord in their lives, but all in the key of pun!

This collection of story-based wordplays is a reflection of me; I have drawn inspiration from a diversity of life experiences. I began writing this work in the summer of 2007 and completed the first draft in about a month. After a few edits, lots of encouragement from friends and family, and outstanding mentorship and faith, I am fortunate to see this work published. While it was not my original intent, I view this work as a form of edutainment. It is natural that my work would fall in the educational realm, as I was raised by a school teacher. I hope that this book will be used by students (young and old) to enhance their vocabulary in an enjoyable way and to increase their desire to pursue lifelong reading and learning. Having spent half of my life on a college campus has certainly stimulated my desire to continue pursuing knowledge, and I hope others discover the same passion. By interacting with so many exceptionally bright people over the years, I have discovered my creative self. Somewhere in the world of pun between Shakespeare and Martin Lawrence, you'll find me. This project was fun to complete, and I hope you find joy in reading it.

The book is divided into several chapters. The first chapter, "Their Eyes Were Watching Job," is a collection of stories in an occupational setting or regarding a business transaction. "I Think Yet I Cram" features tales of students and teachers and, more generally, intellectual high jinks. The third chapter, "Empty Cow or Rheas: I Love My Shakes Pear," is, as you'd imagine, a collection of tales involving food; although it should be noted that these wordplays have little or no nutritional value. The final chapter, "I've Been Around: Whirled without End," features stories of characters in motion.

Seriously, without further, I do. The daze of comedic destruction is a pun, us, and I am back on track.

CHAPTER 1

Their Eyes Were Watching Job

||||||||||||||||||||||||||

Nathan Notall sent companies his credentials on a cushion in the hope that his application would stand out. A potential employer called Nathan to comment that it was unnecessary for him to pad his resume.

Woodrow, a teenager, strolled to his local convenience store, where he encountered the proprietor, Mr. Tuffmann. The owner made an inquiry regarding the young man's post–high school plans. Woodrow explained that he had been accepted to a trade school and planned on becoming a well-respected plumber. The curmudgeon attempted to thwart the vision of this ambitious young man and encouraged him, in order to avoid disappointment, to pipe down on his dreams.

An older lady, Mrs. Brees, had a poorly installed air-duct system in her house. However, because the original manufacturing company had gone out of business, she had no one to which she could vent her frustrations.

Sebastian Sobrunner was really into watching the creative animated commercials on television, particularly the more realistic ones. He found himself drawn to one of the characters, an attractive woman, and during a fit of brave delusion, he attempted to contact her to see if she would pencil him in.

Jason Filmer, a prominent Hollywood writer, wrote a screenplay about a group of daring barbers who moonlight as bank robbers. The film, Cut and Run, was praised by critics and enjoyed by audiences as a stimulating, hair-raising tale.

Sally Sundries, a talented entertainer, decided to perform a complicated and exotic contortionist act during her audition for a renowned traveling revue. She wanted the job desperately and was willing to do almost anything to try to get a leg up on the competition.

Timothy Glass was an annoying window repairman. From the time he arrived at a client's house, he would make idle chatter throughout the duration of his work. He started to lose business as he became a known pane with which to deal.

Tori Branch was a local tree trimmer who had quite a negative reputation for her business practices. She charged full price, but often did only half of the agreed-upon work. Over time, she developed an incredibly shady reputation.

Nathan Cretecone was an exceptional handyman. A crowd of onlookers once witnessed him lay tile for five bathrooms in one hour. Needless to say, they were floored.

Penelope Decker, a worker at a construction company, asked her supervisor how much material it would take to finish the sidewalk project on which they were working. She was frustrated with her supervisor's flighty responses. What she wanted was a more concrete answer.

Paula Penn had worked as an anime artist for years. She got a job working on a major studio's cartoons, and her employers quickly discovered that she was adept at creating and illustrating the stories' endings. Paula truly had a passion for her work and found profit in her tendency to be too quick to draw conclusions.

The carpenters union was having a disagreement about standard wages. J.W.Wood, one of the veteran workers, thought it best to form a special subcommittee to hammer things out.

Jon Sole Lowe interviewed for a corporate position at a prominent company specializing in the sale of tennis sneakers. After reviewing his resume, the hiring manager told him that with his credentials, he was a shoo-in for the job!

At the end of the game that marked the conclusion of his career, Quenton Batt threw his hat into the stands at the urging of the crowd. One fan in a post-game news report commented, "I think it was a nice way to cap things off!"

Cora Lands, a workaholic landscaper, kept up her professional intensity by making compost for hours on end. Finally, the operation's proprietor came outside and told her she should take a break, as she was doing way too mulch.

Pirate Petey Booty moonlighted as a songwriter. Ironically, he always had trouble coming up with hooks for his songs.

After receiving some seemingly outrageous bills, Sam Skinner ventured to have a conversation with his dermatologist, Dr. Rich Pore. Sadly, their talk didn't help clear things up.

Elijah Goode worked hard his entire life to become the best baseball player he possibly could be, and his intense fervor led him to a minor league batting championship prior to his reaching the big leagues. After his retirement, he decided to strike out and redirect his energy into producing his own music album. Ironically, he never had a hit.

Suzanne Roap had always been recognized amongst her peers and coaches as having exceptional strength and, in fact, she led her high school to a championship as a tug-of-war anchor. She later went on to become the president of the labor union for her company. She was primarily elected because her colleagues figured she would have a lot of pull.

Museum curator Billy Write was giving a lecture on antique pens, and he accidentally stuck one of the audience members. The affected member of the crowd just shook her head and noted he need not do that just to get a point across.

Athletic trainer Amy B. Quik was giving a very graphic talk on abdominal physiology and fitness training at a local physical therapist's office. One of the attendees, Samantha Skerritt had to leave the room after a couple of minutes, as she couldn't stomach it.

Jeffrey Toss gave a marketing presentation using specially designed aerodynamic baseballs, and he demonstrated their effects by throwing off of a mound. The audience was wowed by his precise demonstrations; as a former hurler himself, he developed a strong reputation throughout his region for his amazing sales pitch.

An older gentleman, Hampton Saif, worked security overnight at a local bank. Every morning, he would come home exhausted, but his long-winded wife would try to hold a conversation with him as he attempted not to doze off. She was essentially keeping her guard up.

Roberta Romper's dad traveled forty weeks a year as a salesman for a large technology corporation. Roberta often acted out in school, and the wise principal learned the absence of her father was the root of the problem, although that was not initially a parent.

Ms. Teek worked at a mortgage bank with awful management. Slowly but surely, all of her colleagues left. One day, she was the only one working, and the line of applicants wound outside of the building. The customers were upset with the egregious amount of time they spent standing in line. It's no wonder; she was the lone officer there!

Barber Sam Kutright is truly adept with a comb and scissors and is popular all over town because of his good work. He asked one of his teenage clients, Stuart Smartus, for feedback. The young man remarked that while overall he was an excellent stylist, it wouldn't hurt for him to brush up on his clipper techniques.

Writer Marianne Page used to brew her own beer in her spare time. Her specialty was a beverage that included a secret, sandy substance in the recipe. She was a firm believer in her rough draft.

Magazine editor Sheila Letterson hired a young, new-to-the-workforce receptionist, Donna Fingers. Even after Donna found out that the company only used old typewriters to write copy, she was still keyed up about her first job!

A young man, Bobby Cover, used to meticulously install Venetian-style window coverings in houses, a job too painstaking for the average contractor. Nonetheless, he was blind to the fact that he had a very difficult job.

Contractor Katina Cousins was awarded a job installing doors on new construction in residential areas. She was okay until she got to the knobs, a difficult task for her; she just couldn't seem to get a handle on things.

A heavy-set man, Branch Butts, went to the doctor for his physical, and as he was having his weight checked, a five-dollar bill fell out of his back pocket. His doctor quickly dismissed this occurrence, as he figured that Branch was trying to tip the scales.

An old African man, Mr. M'fume, owned an antique store, where he sold, for the most part, old percussion instruments from his native land. When things were slow, he would send all his workers out onto the streets to see if they could drum up some business.

A truck driver, Devin Wheeler, couldn't find the scales at the inspection checkpoint. The truth is that he was unable to find his weigh-in.

Several real estate developers got together frequently to collaborate on their upcoming project. They decided that they should have one more meeting so that their plans for the sidewalks in the development could be set in stone.

Electrician Kiefer Volt passed his customer the bill for his afternoon of work. It was about three hundred dollars more than expected. Needless to say, his client was shocked.

Onetime bandmates Timothy Rocker and Steve Forte argued for years. A promoter managed to get them into a room together, where they both agreed to do a reunion tour; the ultimate goal was to end their careers on a high note.

Electrical worker Wayne Ohm became bored with his mundane days on the job. He researched some good hobbies, as he was looking for another outlet for his energy.

Master carpenter Marjorie Woodson attended city hall meetings on a regular basis. One evening, she curiously kept bringing in stools from her shop. A councilman thought she had political motives behind this action and wondered if her long-term goal was to chair the meeting.

Circus performer Rupert Roper used to eat paper fasteners throughout his act. Based on the awesome audience reaction he received, this portion of the show became a staple of his repertoire.

Buxom blonde bartender Betsy Brewha always received better tips than the rest of her colleagues since she served her drinks in huge glasses with her picture on the side. She always knew that she would get ahead of the game because of her cup size.

Champion racehorse Marty Mare went on a daytime talk show and revealed a great deal about his upbringing in a single-parent household. His mother did the best she could to put food on the table though times were often rough, and he said it was difficult to live in a fodder-less environment.

Hot-air-balloon operator Dana Ball was always aware of the fact that it was better to put a little more propane than was needed for a trip rather than less. She was good about airing on the side of caution.

Union leaders and employees were present at the Snuff City Chamber of Commerce meeting to discuss the prevalence of black lung amongst the coal workers and others in the region. Association leader Smokey Sheppard was adamant about having the attention of all his coworkers, and he stressed this talk was clearly more than a miner discussion.

Cartoonist Edward Bar decided to become an attorney at the height of his career. His transition to the courtroom was smooth since he was already good at illustrating his points.

Private Jones was bold in his professional requests. Having developed a passion for aircraft as a teenage pilot, he told his commander that he wanted to fly—plane and simple.

Farmer Barnes was attempting to hire summer interns. In order to screen them, he decided to see which ones would do the best job at pulling wild plants out of the field. He thought that this would be the best way to weed them out.

Don's Dry Cleaner employee Elroy Rhodes had been a content worker for many years. He recently became disgruntled with the way management was treating his colleagues and wanted to share his story with as many members of the media as possible. Ultimately, he decided not to press the issue.

Burial-site owner Gordon Graves needed to know the layout of new land he had purchased. He realized that the appeal of a park had much to do with the aesthetic arrangement of the spaces. After consulting a friend, he determined what he really needed to do was plot things out.

One of the newest postal workers in town, Stacey Stamps, went to her boss concerning the extreme number of hours she had been working lately. She felt she was becoming enveloped by her job.

Jenny Fingers was a grooming expert who took great pride in her professional efficiency. One of her colleagues encouraged her to enter a local contest for manicurists. She took first place in the speed division since she was able to trim nails at an unbelievable clip.

After their tow-motors malfunctioned, the factory workers had to roll the wheel rims from one end of the building to the other. It was quite a tiring task.

The CEOs of several liquor production companies got together to discuss the possibility of diluting their beverages. All of a sudden, the chair of the meeting, Langston Lakes, stood up and shouted that he was growing weary of all of this watered-down conversation.

The leaders of the woodworkers' association were attempting to arrange a meeting of all of the leaders in the region. However, they could not seem to nail down a date.

Jerome Jarson was planning a long career at the local soup company. Unfortunately, after his third year there, he got canned.

While most neurologists in the hospital were anxious about performing a new procedure, Dr. Rivera did not hesitate; he had plenty of nerve.

At a company staff meeting, President Portante instructed one of his VPs to display a picture of him with a furious face on a video screen. Some of the workers found out about this and were decidedly upset that their boss would project his anger in this fashion.

At the retirement party of television executive Tico Thomas, he mentioned that even though he had enjoyed his time at the company, he thought that it was time to channel his energy in another direction.

Local ice-cream shop owner Barron Butters was involved in an apparent scandal, but no one was able to give the newspaper writers the scoop on it.

Egbert Eckso worked for a company that repaired electrical outlets. His boss noticed that during monthly training sessions, Egbert would doze off. One day after the meeting, the boss told him that he needed to be more plugged-in to what was going on.

Local man Stewart See would peek into the office of CPA Ronnie Record every morning. One cold day, Stewart pressed his face up to the window as usual, and it became stuck there. Ronnie wanted to go outside and help the man, but he remembered that Stewart had become a pane in the glass.

The city council subgroup met the first Monday of every month, and they all had personalized chairs to sit on. Unfortunately, a janitorial service came by on the wrong day to clean the seats and took them away. They decided to proceed with the meeting in any event. Still chairless after two grueling hours, Mayor Mayorga dubbed them a standing committee.

Cardiologist Mena Marshall read several medical journal articles every night before she went to bed. She was determined to keep a finger on the pulse of what was going on in the field.

Kevin Kernal could have easily claimed that the back of his foot was injured in the accident to draw more money from the insurance company. After much thought, however, he decided that he did not want be a heel.

Studio musician Will Wrightnote missed several recording sessions due to the fact that he was dealing with heart palpitations. Will recovered quickly, and he did a great job on his first day back, seeming to not even miss a beat.

Several soldiers were planting explosives into the ground. General Diggs was an experienced munitions expert, and the members of the company asked if he would provide them with advice. He respectfully replied that he wouldn't mine.

Jerry Joicer was working as an intern at an oil field, and his boss wanted him to check on the progress of drilling at several sites. After a few hours, Jerry checked in with his supervisor and reported that everything was going well.

The coat factory workers were chatting so much on the line that it was drastically slowing down production. The shift manager finally approached and told them to zip it.

Gate maker Garry Gardens was fed up with the politics at his company. He was a dedicated worker and had even been named employee of the year recently. Nonetheless, he decided it was high time to post his resignation.

The clock store had been burglarized three times in the past year, so during the staff meeting, proprietor Tammy Ticker told the employees that she was going to put someone on watch.

Most of the people at the baby-product retail company knew that Wesley would suck up to the regional managers. Few realized that the company had brought him in to be a pacifier.

Three young actors had recently joined the union. The trio was invited to a costume party and decided to go as Oscar statues. As soon as they arrived, everyone knew that they were gilded.

Stuart Staples took on a few independent contractors to do maintenance on his building. They would only be working on the top two floors since the bottom levels were already managed by someone else. These new workers turned out to be highered help.

Judge Jacoby was a well-known courtroom manager. He became known for his strict, but fair, judgments in a number of high-profile cases. Unfortunately, he brought a great deal of unwanted attention to himself when he became known for trying to court his counsel.

Dr. Davidson ran a cosmetic surgery clinic in the city. A beautiful woman came to the office for an augmentation consultation; she had just moved to the United States from abroad. He was very upfront with her when he told her that he was not too excited about working with implants.

Mary Martest landed a job in sales at a large hardware store downtown. Her colleagues were, for the most part, a collection of socially awkward twentysomething guys. She quickly went to her boss to hand in her resignation, telling him that she did not really enjoy working with tools.

Reginald Rahmien was promoted to a senior vice president position in a large chowder company in New England. He called his family with the news, and everyone thought that was souper.

Suzanne Saimoe worked for a company that sold letterhead. After lots of hard work, having spent eight years on the job, she was overlooked for a promotion. She contemplated quitting, as she had grown tired of working in such a stationery position.

Lillie Ladel's brother, who did contract work, told Lillie that he was very good at repairing wiring issues. One day on her job, she heard a coworker say that she needed a few such things done around the house, and she decided to take that opportunity to plug her brother.

Chase Chalmer was known to make excessive inquiries of his colleagues and management during the monthly meetings of the Atlantic Mud Mask Manufacturing Company. He was also quick to brag about his connection to a former English prince, and he intentionally stirred things up. Due to this fact, he was considered a roil pain amongst his peers.

Damon Dertminer was a tremendous car salesman but also a known fibber. The owner of a large luxury-car dealership interviewed Damon for a sales position on his lot. The owner knew that hiring Damon would be a risk but was comfortable with his potential lie ability.

Scandal erupted when it was discovered that the defendant in a legal case, the owner of a large, international trucking company, had, as a means of bribery, special tractors built for each juror. In essence, his defense team was attempting to jury-rig the decision.

Billie Jean Bosick used to work at the gateway to a bridge connecting two states, collecting money for the state government. She was not the energetic young lady she had been twenty years ago. The job had taken quite a toll on her.

A large clothing company sent much of their work overseas to save on labor costs. It was later discovered that very young children were slaving away in this operation, responsible for putting most of the color in the shirts and jeans. Marina, a community activist, decided to write a letter to the company; she was upset that in that factory, a child dyes every twenty seconds.

Well-to-do real estate agent Lorton Landess had a number of listings in one of the most expensive neighborhoods in town. He would take some of the interested buyers out to the properties, all the while exhaling cigar smoke. While describing the homes, he would often exaggerate dimensions. On one tour, a customer politely asked him if he would refrain from puffing.

Xavier Zoobill claimed that he could complete any task known to man. His colleagues would offer him many opportunities to fix, for a fee, things around their houses, cars, and so forth. He usually succeeded in the end but would often get stuck on a task and, frustrated, he would curse loudly. Due to his behavior, he became known around the office as a jack of all tirades.

After an avian flu scare, a man who used rent his messenger birds out to businesses to transmit information was approached by his clients to see if his pigeons might actually be carriers of disease.

Some seafood industry executives came together to discuss the toxicity of shellfish in the region. Morally opposed to the thought of potentially offering a soiled product to the public, a few threatened to leave the board and the business altogether. After a few hours of discussion, some of the individuals got heated, and a mediator told them that there was no need for a clam-or-us discussion.

Stuckey Sun was hired by a man accused of hunting an endangered animal species. In protest, Aurelius, a known animal-rights activist and fellow partner at the firm, sat in the break room on top of the client, Shooter's, pertinent files, and Stuckey angrily asked him to get off of his case!

Eunice Eubanner went to a local bank to see if she could qualify for a mortgage to make an offer on a house she liked. Corby, one of the loan officers there, was struck by her beauty when he met with her. She came back to the bank the next day to follow up with him, and he told her she would be able to secure a loan, but it would be based on interest only.

Banker Bix Baggrab was approached by a team of entrepreneurs that desired to borrow funds to start a touring burlesque show. Though the banker thought their idea had substance, he passed on making the loan since it was pretty risqué business.

Evander Ellerwand, a neighborhood handyman, used a special solution to rid his customers' closets of cloth-eating insects. He was also known to have a knack for predicting the future. The local newspaper wrote an article about his intriguing antics, referring to his predictions as "mothman prophecies."

Sonny Smartray's stockbroker told him to think about investing in a company that sold an innovative lat pulldown machine. He was excited, but after speaking with his wife, he decided to back out of the deal.

At Knight's World, a store dedicated to medieval warfare, they periodically hired Frederick Fiefray, a local enthusiast, to coordinate the staging of archaic battles. He was not an employee of the store but appreciated the opportunity to work as a free lancer.

Hector worked in construction and told his coworkers that his grandfather had developed the instrument to determine the horizontal nature of lines on a surface. During lunch, his friend Peyton proudly supported his buddy in this claim. Hector, knowing he had lied, pulled Peyton aside and told him that he needed to level with him.

Corporal Benson was demonstrating to Private Jefferson the technique for loading and unloading an automatic weapon. The corporal showed the private where the chamber for storing the rounds was, and Private

Jefferson mentioned that it looked like something he had seen in a magazine.

Nina Nannada was looking to invest in some property by the beach. Her real estate agent showed her a house a couple of blocks from the water. She liked the place but told the agent that she was looking for more of a shore thing.

Brandon Beanvette loved working on cars. In fact, he loved it so much that he would start shaking if he went a few hours without messing around in the shop. One day while on vacation with his family, he couldn't stand it any longer. He ran up to a local repair shop to see if they would let him get his fix!

Several centuries ago, Wilhelm Workuss, a feudal lord, wanted to determine why all of his tenants were so unified against him. He suspected that they all came from the same family. He did a little research and discovered that their ability to circulate opposition was due to the fact that they were in fact blood vassals.

Alvin Axewell had been riding horses for years, but one day he fell off and developed a phobia for riding. From then on, he did mainly administrative work at the stable and supervised the accounting. In an effort to motivate him to start riding again, the owner approached him and asked if he tired of living life as a desk jockey.

Bee queen Busy Buzzelda reprimanded one of her colony who was known to go out drinking and then shout obscenities. She threatened to have his vocal cords removed, and he was frightened about the prospect of having his buzz taken away.

Prince Pearbow was an outstanding communicator. However, he was known to have unwieldy handwriting. He was at the office of his landlord, Mr. Herndon, who knew this fact. As Prince was about to write out his payment, Mr. Herndon told him to make sure keep it in check.

The Cheatham Agency was hosting a comedy competition for up-and-comers in the area. They saw a wide range of talent, but by the end, the comics were all equally solid, most of them doing at least one quirky impersonation. The judges agreed that at that point, the competition had reached a state of parody.

Jimmy Jumpagain was in the business of designing contemporary stackable bunk beds. He wanted to sell over a million units. His agent told him that, though possible, it was quite a lofty goal.

Bethany, a professional pickpocket who lived in a small residential area downtown, would flirt with some of the guys in the vicinity by talking seductively and batting her eyes at them. After awakening from their trance, they would often notice their wallets missing. A group of them got together to talk about what to do since they were tired of being hoodwinked.

Myra Moonbow was a beautiful clothier of both Native American and Latin descent. Malcolm was dating her, but he decided to end the relationship since he was suspicious that she was sending him mixed signals.

CHAPTER 2

I Think Yet I Cram

◇◇◇◇◇◇◇◇◇◇

Many of Larry Leffer's friends were planning on attending the regional southpaw convention this past weekend. This event had earned a reputation as one of the most enjoyable events in the area. Being appropriately physically inclined, Larry decided to go since he didn't want to get left out of all of the fun.

Schizophrenic Seamus Tuman was known to get flustered when it rained. His doctor took him away from the mental hospital for some fresh air, but when he saw a thunderstorm approaching, the doctor quickly turned around. He didn't want to do anything that would precipitate this guy's anger.

Spencer Spaulder was a tightly wound, analytical person. He had a habit of worrying himself into a state of utter fatigue. In fact, any time he had a problem, he would go take a nap. His wife commented to a friend how great it was for Spencer to be able to put his issues to rest.

Mr. Chandler, the principal at a local elementary school, was a big advocate of fire safety. However, one of the parents noted at a PTA meeting that the seventy-five fire drills he initiated during the course of an academic year were excessive and quite alarming.

In a recent quiz bowl tournament, a group of sailors played against army officers. In a bit of irony, it was the seamen that seemed to always be fishing for answers.

One of the coordinators of an adhesive convention, Danny Duct, was asked to jump into one of the displays while someone filmed him for a commercial. His biggest concern was the fact that he didn't want to be on tape.

A marathon runner, Jennifer Anne Miles, needed to go to the psychologist for some mental training. She was asked to recall some specific races and could not. The shrink did everything he could to jog her memory.

A trigonometry how-to show on public access television is hosted by a controversial and questionably clad local math teacher. Many concerned parents describe the highly rated program as being much too graphic for area youth.

A mischievous young couple was doing community service in a library, and as part of their work, the pair was asked to restock the books. The librarian offered her assistance, but they hastily responded, "No. We want to do it by our shelves."

As a prank, some of Billy Bardo's delinquent schoolmates tied him to the motor of an abandoned car. He stayed there for several days before he was discovered. A few years later, in his teens, he decided to write a book about his days in the hood.

The private instructor at a popular local yoga studio, Mary Matt, was popular amongst her corporate clients. They were always pressed for time, but she was always flexible in her scheduling.

Dean Richards instructed students how to set up arrow signs to direct kids to a special program on campus. Unfortunately, most of them never got the point.

After speaking with her academic advisor, Bobbie Booker determined that politics should be her major. At the meeting, they also contemplated whether or not Bobbie should have a second concentration in history. This was no minor discussion.

Jason Jewel, a recently graduated MBA, was attempting to start a business but did not have a great amount of start-up capital. An older couple looking to retire decided to sell their donut shop to him for a substantially discounted price, and Jason was pretty excited about the prospect of such a sweet deal.

The students in a nursing course were charged with the responsibility of doing a research paper on baby beds. In a scandalous turn of events, a school newspaper reporter discovered that much of the nursing students' work was cribbed.

At his graduation speech, Marvin Mezzo mentioned that the piano teacher he'd worked with from age five had been instrumental in his success.

Klaus Klimer decided to take powerlifting as an elective. He thought it might help his GPA since it was, in fact, a weighted course.

Nicole Nolege's professor told her that a grant allowed the class to spend the last two weeks of the semester studying offshore on a cruise liner with students from other colleges. Her dream had come true, and she quickly called her mother to explain that she would finally be studying on a scholar ship.

Dudley Detmine was one of the smartest guys around. He would enter national trivia contests, often answering every single question correctly. Last night, however, when he went to a local contest, the emcee asked a question about trees. It was one of the rare times that a question stumped him.

A group of lead-footed librarians were caravanning to a conference, and a cop, Bertha Badger, pulled them over for reckless driving. Instead of allowing them to arrive at their intended destination, Officer Badger took them all to the station to be booked.

University math professor Art Plotter challenged the class to see who could work out the most mathematical distribution problems over the course of a twenty-four-hour period. A few of them were concerned, as that would truly test their limits.

Private music instructor Terry Treble decided to have a few sessions with all of his students. He was a crusader for group learning, and he thought that they would all work well together. As it turned out, this was only true in theory.

Mark Mathis volunteered at the local Boys and Girls Club as a tutor. He was fun, as he would wear a white T-shirt and let the kids work out simple problems on it in marker. Unlike many of the other volunteers, he always showed up for his session. Mark was the type of volunteer everyone could count on!

The midcentral state women's swim team, the Crescents, thought it would be a great prank to paint their backsides with their team logo and colors, blue and white. Then they exposed themselves to the audience before the swim meet they were hosting. It was the type of thing you see once in a blue mooning.

Sally's stats teacher would always call on her to quickly compute the averages for a series of numbers. Mr. Mayhue was known to be exceptionally demanding, and these interactions with Sally were thought to be mean tactics.

Adrien Ambosh, the class bully, would walk by Stephen every morning and stick him in the side with his ballpoint. By the end of the school year, Stephen had a great deal of penned-up anger.

A summer art class was working on creating the largest horse statue in the state. They had been working on the animal's rear end for at least forty-eight hours. The instructor approached the group and told them that they needed to hurry since they were two days behind.

Cheryl Cabella wrote her book in clean, southwestern Virginia air. When she went to a more densely populated location to put the finishing touches on it, she found that the atmosphere made her hazy.

Part of Alexis Alto's comprehensive final exam for her graduate program in meteorology was to demonstrate the use of a barometer in front of the faculty committee. She cracked under the pressure.

Jake Drawtup wanted to start receiving input from his audience to help him write his mysteries. He took this idea to his publisher, and she thought it was a novel idea.

Joshua approached his history professor, Dr. Meant, and told him that his lecture on the history of dollar bills made no cents at all.

Mrs. Gunner had her sixth-grade class write their favorite original slogans on poster board and create borders using nickels and dimes. Her goal was to help them learn how to coin phrases.

Young cartographer Chris Corners sat down with his mentor often to talk about life and work. Chris found these conversations extremely valuable. Last week, he needed some strong career advice, so the two of them met to map out Chris's plans.

Francisco Fortunato, an older monk, would invite in the younger brethren and give them philosophy lectures over assorted tempura. Because of these meetings, Francisco became known to his contemporaries as the deep friar.

A kindergarten teacher had her children take rests in the middle of the day. Not a fan of long hair on boys, she would often try to trim it during that time, but some of the students would awaken feeling startled. The principal caught wind of this and told the teacher that she was not happy about having the kids' naps cut short.

Petra Porto, an out-of-the-box thinker, decided that she would enlighten her classmates with her off-the-cuff discussions about psychic energy. The rambling discussions did not impress her classmates. They were barely loose id.

James Jammer had distinguished himself as a scientist and was given the ultimate award for his work, the opportunity to travel on a space mission. When he returned from his moon mission, he noticed a bump on his arm. He went into the laboratory to have it checked out. It turns out he was bitten by a lunar tick.

At a national PC convention, one exhibitor demonstrated an early model computer whereby a man in a buggy would travel across the screen if the processor stalled. The representative referred to this man as the computer's internal driver.

The agricultural students at the local college were assigned the task of writing reports on the history of popcorn consumption in movies. Due to the large amount of conflicting information, it was hard for many of the students to find relevant kernels of truth.

An elementary school teacher, Ms. Thomas, wanted her students to walk into the rink single file for their private demonstration on professional roller-skating. She was a little frustrated about it, as she thought they would never get in-line.

Sandra Shavers, in her third year of college, was having a rough time balancing her studies with her professional figure-skating career. After her second consecutive semester of academic mediocrity, her dean told her that she was on thin ice.

At the regional actuary conference, the leader was trying to figure out ideal group sizes for the attendees to work in teams. He thought that six was reasonable, and his assistant leader told him that was a perfect number.

A manufacturer of office supplies got the team of scientists together to have a large brainstorming session on how to build a better ballpoint. After an hour of deep thought, he grew tired of being so pensive about the matter.

The Navy Seals were on a boat, required to complete a communication course prior to returning to land. The students were separated; the best were taught on the top deck, while the remedial pupils remained on the first level. Omar was upset, as he thought the admiral mistakenly put him in the wrong group. He was opposed to being a part of the low class.

Gawky nerd Gary Gruber developed a new game of wits, whereby opponents squared off with each other. The winner of each round earned the right to make a new rule for the game, written on a block of concrete and posted on top of a wall. The game became highly popular with geeks and was known to the common crowd as the Rube Bricks.

Shauna Sakefore was attempting to research the history of anesthesia and consulted her professor about some good sources of information. Shauna's instructor told her that she might see if she could dig up a few good nuggets on the ether net.

Kaleb Koolburch went to Professor Li's dinner and discussion event, which the professor had advertised for his course on advanced Chinese literature. Kaleb got the days mixed up and instead attended the professor's remedial language course, along with several dozen students at the college. This scholar was expecting the lo mein he was served but did not expect to encounter such a dim sum.

Mr. Bellbate was asked by his friend, a business professor, to give the students a talk on the development of his oil refinery. All Mr. Bellbate proceeded to do was talk about his family's great wealth, created in the petroleum business. At the end of the hour, the students wondered why Professor Waite would subject them to such a gassy lecture.

Chloe Cortoe, a mischievous child, periodically spit water from the drinking fountain onto her classmates. The teacher informed her mother of the cherub's wrongdoings, and Chloe was subsequently grounded. Her father called back to get an update on her behavior a couple of weeks later, and the teacher informed him that although the mischievous behavior was not regular, Chloe still did it in spurts.

Trina Toestep was on the double Dutch team, and she and her friends would sneak away from their classes at the local junior high in order to practice. Her father was upset when the principal called the house in order to inform him that Trina had been school skipping.

Dr. Carrion was honored with a dinner ceremony for his groundbreaking research on the release of atomic energy. At the event, the host introduced him as a true fissionary.

One of the sections of an introductory English course at a small liberal arts college was dropped due to an instructor having to go on medical leave. When he reached campus after an eye appointment, Professor Writewell was surprised to find that the students from the canceled section had been added to his course. He was shocked to find that his pupils had been dilated.

Wellington Wallwear, a well-known tailor, was hired by a fashion school to give a talk to the students about the history of sleeves for men's dress apparel. Since important school officials and other industry notables would be in attendance, he decided not to give the lecture off-the-cuff.

Cynthia Clarevoyage chose the Dog Star to present as a part of a project for her intermediate astronomy course. Several of her classmates started daydreaming during her talk, and she told them to pay attention; her presentation was Sirius business!

Matisse and her friend Leila witnessed a fight at school between two of their female classmates. Matisse, known to exaggerate, told their mutual friend, Suzie, about the fight, saying that it started with the classmates making rude comments to each other and then escalated into a bloodbath. Leila chimed in to say that although the argument was intense, she wouldn't say it fell into that catty gory.

Arielle Ariestar had written lyrical poems for years, but she hadn't received a check from her publisher in several months. She approached her manager to see if he would help her collect her ode money.

Mr. Waechter, the band director at a local middle school, was teaching his students about embouchure. They were eager to learn and wanted to continue practicing after the hour was over. The students objected to his command, so he told them that he didn't want any more lip!

Leo Larnyard, a former inmate at a state prison, decided that he wanted to write a book about his experience. He visited several publishers to see if they would give him a book deal. One publisher was interested in reading a draft to better understand the con text.

Ward was proud of his daughter, Suzie. She was perfect in every way, with accomplishments as a champion rower and an academic scholar. However, she did have one flaw; she was very indecisive. Ward took her on a fun kayaking trip to help her be more decisive. At the outfitter, the cashier asked whether Suzie preferred shorter or longer paddles. Ward smiled in excitement as this was the either-oar type of scenario he wanted her to be able to work through.

Meghan Knott was a pediatric nurse who loved the kids she treated. An educational researcher, Timmy Turnpage, visited the hospital and tried to administer SATs to the children in an attempt to link illness with aptitude performance. Meghan caught Timmy on a couple of occasions and asked him politely not to return. On the third instance, she got really annoyed, as it had really started to test her patients.

Sissy Scratchwrite was quite an imaginative writer, especially considering the fact that she was only ten years old. The only problem, in her teacher's eyes, was that she would occasionally and unnecessarily slip in some foul language. Before their next assignment was due, Mr. Robinson had a talk with Sissy and said that he did not want her to use any cursive writing this time.

Josephine Junelow was collecting exotic animals from all over the world and planned on opening up a small zoo to educate people about the existence of these animals. Mr. Fences, a well-known philanthropist, decided to donate five of his Himalayan goats to her. She called to thank him and told him that his contribution was tahr-rific.

The hospital administrators considered babies born under the last sign of the zodiac calendar to be lucky. The parents of these infants were given a special cobbler in celebration after the mothers had rested. The CEO caught wind of this act and thought that it was unfair to the other parents and told the hospital staff to commence a pie cease.

A mother-to-be was at an outdoor health-care fair run by the local hospital. She was discussing some feeding options with a few of the RNs when it started pouring rain. After getting drenched, the expectant mother continued to speak with them and then abruptly decided that she wanted nothing to do with a wet nurse.

Carson Comma's advisor wondered why Carson was so pressed to complete his cardiology research study. He suspected his advisee had some arterial motives.

Nathan Nawlenz saw some interesting spiders hanging from the outside of his grandmother's house. He and his cousin went to inspect. Nathan, a nature enthusiast, wanted to learn more. His cousin mentioned that in order to get the information he desired, he was going to have to do some research on the web.

Warren Wickersham's friends teased him about the fact that he would go into deep thought over the simplest questions. They thought that their jokes were harmless and funny, but he told them he was not a muse.

Eva Eversuch, a synesthete, thoroughly disliked crimson or any similar colors. Her boyfriend Hans told her that she needed to release her hate red.

CHAPTER 3

Empty Cow or Rheas: I Love My Shakes Pear

||||||||||||||||||||||||||

Alexander Bellepot, an aging, overweight baseball player decided to hang up his cleats as he neared obesity. In the team's waiver letter to him, they cited the fact that he had clearly taken one too many trips to his home plate.

Junie Troutman was once at a Mexican restaurant for dinner, and they brought out a large fish for her consumption, head included. She exclaimed, "Excuse me, sir? This portion of fish is too large. Do you mind bringing out the scaled-down version?"

Bernie Chew was in a local steakhouse and noticed a piece of artwork resembling a guillotine hanging on the wall above his booth. He'd always considered the food at this establishment to be first-rate but hadn't realized that the place was a cut above.

A local greasy spoon cook, Eddie Poacher, decided to enter an omelet-cooking contest. He kept scrambling after the competition was over, as the audience kept egging him on.

Cletus Clamby was the most introverted clam in his family, which included eight other siblings. His concerned mother wanted him to participate in activities that would force him to socialize. After years of effort, she finally gave up, deciding that Cletus couldn't possibly come out of his shell.

Waitress Wilma Dunn attempted to explain to a customer why the steak was overcooked. Wilma was known as a caring but logical server. At the end of the day, her justification did not seem to have a lot of meat in it.

A minor-league baseball team sponsored a fundraiser prior to their game. During the seventh-inning stretch, they had some farm chickens race up the first-base line. All the animal rights groups, however, were crying fowl.

A little town known as Wet Canyon created a dry policy that prevented all drinking establishments from operating. While many in the town were satisfied with this austere ordinance, many were determined to get around it. Food critic Peter Passerby made a brief stop through Wet Canyon on his national tour and noted on his blog that it was one of the lamest places he'd been, bar none.

When a group of farmers met with the president, they only wanted to talk about their cattle instead of the planned topic: the damage pesticides did to their orchards. Frustrated, the head of the organization, Beatrice Bugg, remarked that it was a pretty fruitless conversation.

Renee Remoulade made a cashew chicken dish for her guests, even after discovering that many of them had food allergies. After Renee announced what the entrée was, the whole party was going nuts!

Paul Petris had been searching all year long for an employment situation where he could work once school was out. He was about to take a summer job packaging poultry but heard of many accidents occurring at the plant. After his friends found out that he was not going to take the high-paying job, they told him that he was just too chicken.

Two groups of grapes were engaged in a whiny argument about which owned the property they lived on; the disagreement had gone on for years. Eventually, both sides decided to squash it.

On a scorching summer afternoon, a pack of grapes was accidentally dropped from an airline cargo shipment into the desert. After a couple of days, they started drying out. Next thing anyone knew, the entire lot was raisin' hell.

While reading a great mystery novel, Bob Booker discovered that one of the suspects, Nicholas Knack, had gone on a pretzel-stealing rampage prior to being arrested for larceny. This discovery provided quite a twist at the end of the book!

An army of soda bottles marched the battlefields with confidence. Even amongst these soldiers, there was one bottle that stood tall above the others—Cap Ouncer. For his charismatic qualities, he was named liter of the pack.

Although most of the students passed by the chicken sandwiches that had been sitting under 100-watt bulbs for hours, Joseph quickly grabbed one. He was known to enjoy light snacks.

Andrew Almose and I sat together over lunch. We shared some pie slices, an assortment of types we had ordered. He told me that sharing food was a calming experience for him. I think that he really just desired a piece of mine.

Ricky Roller's mom had to leave the house unexpectedly and told him that he needed to watch the tomatoes simmering on the stove. Since he couldn't go out and play basketball with his friends, this left him stewing.

Two politicians, Senators Cheatham and Slicker, had long been bitter enemies but decided to get together over a porterhouse steak. This seemed to be a good way to get over the beef they'd had for years.

Leigh Lessoni worked in a secret vegetable garden. Prior to her employment, the owner required her to sign a waiver promising not to leek any information.

Bertram Bredder told his employees at Biscuit Heaven that the store would start to sell jars of their signature sausage-based sauce. He said the first twenty or so they sold each day would get them to their break-even point. Anything after that would be gravy!

Elton Eaton almost choked on a bone at the barbecue smokehouse. However, most of his friends were careful not to rib him about it.

Oscar's boss was known for eating a certain type of trail mix. She messily ate this snack during meetings and while writing events on her huge planner. By the time she was done, there were several dates on the calendar.

A group of baseball players went to a restaurant and ordered steak and lobster. It turns out that the filet mignon was not real meat but rather made from soy protein. Once they made this discovery, they asked to not be charged for their meals. The athletes told the restaurant management they were not big fans of artificial turf.

Leah the Lion would always ask God for forgiveness just before pouncing on and subsequently eating her midafternoon snack. Throughout the jungle, Leah became known for praying on other creatures.

Lindsey Lohio would usually let her little brother, Jimmy, squeeze his juice box from the top of the stairs onto her tongue. Unlike in dealing with bullies at school, Lindsey enjoyed this punch in the mouth.

Bubba Boatright was hired to work in the restaurant of a double-decker day-cruise ship. He could not cook or take instructions, but he could use his brawn to help lift the little kids onto the second deck for a playful thrill every once in a while. In the end, Bubba turned out to be nothing more than a dumb waiter.

Head chef Theodore Tumson was known to personally take his creations from the kitchen to his favorite regulars. It was not uncommon for him to share a little local gossip with them while he visited their table. The manager, however, reprimanded Teddy for giving out the daily dish.

Little Jimmy Jingles went to the neighborhood convenience store to buy a pack of his favorite bubble gum. The total always came to $1.04. Each day, he would come in with only a dollar, and the store would spot him the four pennies. After several weeks, the frustrated owner of the store phoned Jimmy's mom and told her that it was time for some change.

Gloria Gatefell would often go out in her garden to lie in her hammock and eat some of her freshly picked snap peas. This activity brought her great tranquility. She told her neighbor that there was nothing like vegging out in her backyard.

Pete Peppers was at a party a couple of weeks ago, and he saw a young lady hanging out alone, peeling the logos off of her glass beverage container. He expressed his concern and mentioned that if something were wrong, she need not keep it bottled up.

A wealthy beverage distributor, Hack Quious, was worried about the most recent quarterly report, which stated that production was down. He was worried about his liquid assets.

Don Dieper, a high school hitting coach, was known locally for having the most outstanding fried chicken recipe in the area. He was going to record a segment for a regional cooking show, using a couple of his players as assistants. Don was all set to film, but he said he needed a better batter so that he could properly demonstrate.

R.J. Barnhoff led a group of farmers who ground and cooked their special sausages at the county fair. He was an excellent cook and was truly passionate about his work. R.J. would typically smile during the entire event and thus became known as the head cheese.

Stephanie Soupress purchased a small pizza for her lunch one day. Her cousin Larry, a known mooch, asked her for some. It was hard to tell if she was agitated, but she expeditiously proceeded to let him halve it!

Beck Beacons used to watch over his family's livestock while sitting on a giant pumpkin. Once, he jumped off of the pumpkin and fell onto one of the family's cows. This occurrence really caught him off gourd.

The owner of a malt-production plant was giving a group of interns a lesson on distribution. Some of them were carrying on a conversation amongst themselves. Disgusted, intern Tabitha Tomero told them to be quiet—she could barley hear.

On a ship in Southeast Asia, a tourist refused to eat while the ship was in motion, as it caused him to be ill. The back-and-forth motion of the vessel was often enough to cause him to vomit. He mentioned to the crew that he was not a big fan of careen food.

Chef Theodore Tummi had spent most of his days lately thinking of the perfect recipe for his lentil soup. Day and night, he had this creation on his mind. His girlfriend had grown weary of such talk and told him not to be such a pea-brain.

Terra Termbook and her sisters were assigned to make fresh bread for the sorority fundraiser. They decided to start baking after a party at which they had partaken of some illegal substances. The bread, which usually bakes for about an hour, was taken out after thirty minutes. The next day, the house mother saw the loaves and was upset to find that they had been half-baked.

Head grocery-store butcher Harvey Hack had a trio of his underlings do an inventory on the number of legs of lamb and pork that had come in during the last couple of days. Wanting to boost morale, he thought of giving these employees a cool group name, so he decided to call them the add hock committee.

Angelina Allegore loved the antique skillet her grandmother passed down to her; it was used to make fried chicken. Angelina was convinced that the cookware was possessed. In every instance, after she used it, something strange would happen in her kitchen. She was certain that the skillet created a certain amount of pan demonium.

Victoria Versatile told her mother that she had developed a tool to turn block cheese into the finest slices possible. Her mom responded, "Oh honey, that's grate."

Zita Zygotha thought that she might have lost her class ring while venturing through the rows of mustard greens in Aunt Ocy's garden. She was distraught, but Aunt Ocy reassured her that the jewelry would turn up.

Lucy Listlove was attempting to squeeze the Grey Poupon out of a bottle onto a chili dog she was about to consume. After several tries, her dad told her to squeeze harder, but all her strength had been mustered.

Every Christmas morning, Uncle Kevin would whip up a nice breakfast for the family, featuring his signature eggs Benedict. Being the punster, he would pour his delectable sauce on the poached eggs and greet each family member with a joyful, "Happy Hollandaise!"

Sister Sarita was cooking a meal for her husband, Brother Barney. She was attempting to help him reduce his weight, and for supper, she fed him one turkey slice and a single roasted chicken leg. Upset, he asked why she had to make such a paltry meal for him.

At a weight-loss camp, the counselors wanted to help the attendees disassociate eating with comfort, so they decided that instead of having them consume their meals at the plush dining table, they would have them eat while sitting on the edge of a sidewalk. The counselors felt that this would be a great way to help the campers curb their appetite.

The directors of three golf centers in town decided that they would have a joint party to celebrate the first day of summer play. One director would serve appetizers. They would then have folks venture to the next center for the main entrée. Finally, the patrons would consume dessert at the last, in what was sure to be a delectable three-course meal.

Ziggy Zongbuoy worked as a chef at a Caribbean restaurant. He was often hard to deal with and sometimes rude to the waitstaff and customers. One day, he offered some of his special spiced meat to Leroy, one of the waiters, who said that he was not interested in eating some jerk's chicken.

Cecilia Cartcomer was in her garden picking cucumbers, and as a practical joke, some of her friends sneaked a hose from a thirty-five-gallon vinegar barrel into the soil. She started to smell the sour scent, and at that point, she knew she was in quite a pickle.

CHAPTER 4

I've Been Around: Whirled
without End

||||||||||||||||||||||||

Klaus Klawdest, an adventuresome soul, would often outdo himself with some of his outrageous exploits. Folks came from miles around just to hear his stories of revelry and mischief. Last night, he became very intoxicated and wore his Excalibur uniform for hours—talk about a night in shining armor!

Ebe and Katrina met at an annual formal dance that was held outside the base lines of a well-known baseball field. The couple ended up getting engaged. It seems like they really hit it off at the Foul Ball!

A group of people were riding in cars along the Bay Bridge-Tunnel, and like dominoes, they took ill. It was one of the worst cases of carpool tunnel syndrome in recent memory.

Whitney Whizzle was doing maintenance on her truck, which she referred to as if it were a human being. One day it wouldn't start, and though she initially thought that it was a battery problem, it turned out "her son" had blown a fuse. Relieved, she replied, "Well, at least he doesn't have a terminal illness."

A group of apprentices was traveling together as future master deep-sea fishermen. They were all in the same boat, learning together. In fact, they were actually on an intern ship.

This past summer, Tourissa McDays was visiting the USSR, and it seemed like the people were always in a hurry to get somewhere. At one point, she yelled, "Why are you all Russian!

Marcus Mohart and a bunch of his military buddies went out for some fun on the town. They barhopped at some local joints and came home after rebelliously and aggressively joyriding some large armored vehicles while chugging beverages. They ultimately got written up by their commanding officer for their canned tankerous behavior.

A few guys in a sailboat tried to call the coast guard when they drifted too far beyond the shoreline during a hurricane; however, the coast guard never got wind of it.

Ivan Blader traveled to see the national championships in fencing. He began starting conversations with others in the audience and asked one gentleman, "Do you like fencing?" The man hesitantly replied, "It's an enjoyable pastime…of swords!"

Suzie Field was an athletic perfectionist. She consistently stressed herself out when she went through hitting slumps on the softball field. When she didn't succeed during the conference tournament, she went over the edge, and one of her coaches suggested that she might have gone completely batty.

An elderly woman, Ms. Head, used to keep her wigs in a chest of drawers, a unique family heirloom. When visitors came into town, she loved to introduce them to her hair dresser.

Ricky Roguer, a known kleptomaniac, broke into baseball stadiums and attempted to sneak away with the bases. Even when he was little, Ricky had aspirations of stealing home.

Jesse Jacobson was an avid outdoorsman and maverick. He never wanted to follow the law in terms of deer hunting, including the ordinance banning gamesmanship on Sundays. He did all he could to get around the policy, and it seemed that all he wanted to do was buck the system.

During the past few months, Sonia Stareson had noticed an unusually large number of men and boys in her town sporting crew cuts. Interviewed for an article on fashion by the local entertainment journal, she commented that this style seemed to be all the buzz again.

Captain Joseph Scales accounted for three hundred pounds of trout caught on their fishing trip, but the dock said that the combined weight was only 220 pounds. The scale confirmed his initial guesstimate, and he just knew there was something fishy about that!

Mrs. Bynaree used to make her bickering twin daughters press their dresses before school. To make it into a competition, she would judge whose clothes were the sharpest. In reality, she was just trying to help them iron out their differences.

Director Theodore Klime refused to let any of us have an early viewing of his movie on mountains. In truth, all we wanted was a little peak.

Olympic swimmer Brielle Pool was asked in an interview to elaborate on the details of her life. The interviewer inquired about a highly scrutinized encounter Brielle had with the law. It was soon clear to the interviewer that based on Brielle's expression that it was not a subject she was eager to dive into.

Two does, Betty and Bertha, were stuck in a canyon in the frozen tundra. The conditions were tough, but they continued to hang on for deer life.

Sammie Adday lived in a country in which the days of the week were referred to in an ordinal fashion; that is, Monday was one, Tuesday two, and so forth. The man felt awkward, as he knew that in a place like this, his days were numbered.

A group of fishermen went out on a boat to look for oysters. They took cases of spirits to enjoy while out on their journey. They caught tons of food and got completely shelled.

Felon Tiny Billy likes to drink straight whiskey out of a coffee cup. After one particular escapade, he told a warden that he needed no help with his profile picture since he was experienced at taking the mug shot.

Little Beth decided to volunteer for a cowboy's lasso-tying demonstration. She did this even though she was slightly apprehensive. The cowboy tied his rope around her waist; needless to say, her stomach was in knots.

Scouts around the league drooled over professional softball prospect Gretchen Grounder. On her days off, she doubled as a successful cosmetic consultant. The scouts loved her for her athleticism and tremendous makeup as a player.

A plane recently went down in the water near a remote island, but fortunately all of the passengers swam safely to shore. There were no inhabitants there, but curiously, there were plants everywhere resembling strawberry shortcake. Prominent newspaper writer Priscilla Penn commented that it surely must have been a desserted island.

A four-hundred-pounder, Antonio Waite, became famous for his tobacco-spitting feats. In fact, he pretty much kept his big mouth packed wherever he traveled. He was a star of tremendous proportion. His fans affectionately called him the Big Dipper.

The Lincoln Lacrosse Club had won fifteen straight games and was very confident going into the championship game. Coach Kelvin Sticks warned them, however, that this was no time to be lax.

A group of robots got together at the gym every morning to work out. They had limited time, so they thought that they would be best served by doing some intense circuit training.

Patty Podd took her sick frog to her priest for prayer. Father Joseph said that the frog could heal, but it was going to take quite a leap of faith.

Momma Martez was a caring woman who supported her family in any of their endeavors. She had high expectations for them and was not afraid to punish her kids, Luis and Christine, after play practice because they didn't know how to act.

Tiffany Ringer and Greg Groom had a serious conversation where they contemplated a marriage to each other in the future. Both of them had a private fear of commitment, but it turns out that the discussion was quite engaging.

A mysterious figure came into the clubhouse and stole all of Tom Tupin's golf balls. There were no good leads on the crime, and needless to say, Tom was quite teed off about it!

Martha Marvell's two-year-old son got into the workroom and ingested several pieces from the toolbox. She took him to the doctor, and several bolts were discovered in his tummy—he could have died from the experience. When Martha's husband arrived home from work, she told him what had happened. It was truly a tough nut for him to swallow.

The pendant from Janet Joler's necklace fell onto the pavement. A little kid, Bobby Botcher, picked up the pendant, a diamond-encrusted piece. As he handed it back to her, he exclaimed that it was off the chain!

Two young men, Paul Peddle and Mark Means, were kayaking down the river. After a few hours, they decided that they should take their boats to land and get a bite to eat. Mark had no money, so Paul said that he would be happy to float him a few dollars.

Cowboy John was considered to be the top belt maker in the Southwest. He was asked to join the staff of an amusement park so that he could make his product in front of all of the visitors. After about an hour on the job, he got extremely nervous and buckled under the pressure.

Alfred Axion got hit in the thigh with a baseball, and it left a strong imprint on his leg. He visited the doctor, who told Alfred that fortunately the injury is not as bad as it seams.

All the boys from a certain neighborhood were now grown up. One Christmas, they played a game of wiffle ball with the same yardstick they used to play with fifteen years ago. This yardstick, affectionately known as Woody, was truly a ruler among men.

Hot hair stylist Hannah Harold works down the street from Jerry Just's house. He has stopped by several times to ask her out on a date, but she always seems to brush him off.

People watched intently as Prince Fernando descended the three hundred steps from the top of the palace. As he approached the ballroom floor, he started to grow tired of all the intense stairs.

Christina Culture often goes to the nail salon, and she typically asks her boyfriend to pay for it. The last time they were in the car, she mentioned that she wanted a pedicure. He immediately wanted to know who was going to foot the bill.

Pitching coach Karl Korner had his players do long-toss drills for hours. He knew that they were in pain but assured them that getting through the throes would pay off in the end.

Micah Micher and Suzie Shurely were playing a marathon Ping-Pong match on a glass table. Due to a sudden temperature change, the table cracked. At least it provided a much-needed break in the action.

Betsy Breaker drove up to the service station to fill up her tank. As the thousandth customer, she received her fuel at no cost. She was totally gassed!

After Karen Karro had competed in several exhibition tennis matches that summer, she called her agent. She wanted to find out what her net pay was.

Derrick's cousin, prize fighter James Jawbrich, asked him if he would come over and help pack his things in containers so that the movers could come and take them over the weekend. Derrick quickly informed James that he was not a big fan of moving, particularly if it involved boxing.

Liam Leggup took groups of tourists all over the country. On a recent visit to a gambling-laced township, he warned his group that going into the casinos and playing the roulette tables all night was a dicey operation.

Cory Callus, a professional body builder, would stare at his bloated, vascular arms in the gym mirrors for minutes on end. Most of the patrons thought the act was completely vain.

Emma spun wool in her spare time but was known to lie about how much she could do in a specific period of time. I told her there was no need to fabricate.

A pledge master told his group of fraternity initiates that they could only walk on the left side of the street. One of the guys voiced his opinion. He was concerned that they were not allowed to have any rights.

Emily's task in the morning was to open all of the gates at the amusement park. It was considered a mundane task, and no one seemed to know why she got so keyed up about it.

Two explorers, Sandy Sunback and Cam Mullump, were lost in the desert. The hot, intense sunlight continually shone on their faces to the point that they were often hallucinating. These conditions continued for daze.

Elmer Eden was one of the most prolific hunters around, and his living room resembled a taxidermy museum. He would bring the ladies by to impress them. Everyone in town knew that Elmer had lots of game.

Dom Desten, the head athletic trainer, was teaching the star quarterback some new deltoid exercises. In his second set, the athlete tore the rotator cuff of his throwing arm. The athletic department was extremely upset about the injury. Dom ended up having to shoulder the blame for the injury.

Reba Ready found an online pattern for a bird costume she was going to sport to a party. At the last minute, however, she decided to wing it.

Toby Tupper was excited about purchasing a brand new skillet for his mother on her birthday. Unfortunately, the store had sold out of the most popular model. As Toby was visibly upset, the clerk told him to not be so down even though things didn't pan out.

Relief pitcher Ronald Runners was in the dugout with his teammates on a long road series, and they were in the midst of a sweltering afternoon game. Since it was his day off, Ronald was attempting to help cool the guys off between innings by waving towels in front of their faces. His manager told him that he should not be trying to fan his own batters.

Every Saturday morning, Stefan and his brother, Arthur, were assigned the chore of dusting the living room furniture. Stefan, the oldest, would typically start them off by tossing a dustcloth on top of Arthur's head. After many weeks, Arthur protested, decidedly upset that he'd been ragged on.

In his newest film, director Jeremy Joggon ended the story with a man talking to his lover while holding onto the edge of a cliff with one hand. Afraid, the man's lover looks down helplessly from above. Critics believed it to be one of the most gripping films in recent memory.

Bebe Backon was devastated to discover herself and the husband she had divorced in compromising modeling photos posted on the Internet. Even though they were no longer together, the two remained friends. She was upset to find the images of her ex posed.

The most recent blockbuster, a horror film, includes several scenes in which the main characters are graphically wounded. Lisa Lightner, who was only thirteen, told her older cousin that she did not want to see any more scarry movies.

Fledgling hip-hop artist Felicia Flow had been in the music business for many years. She decided to increase her notoriety by recording a song about some of the mistakes made by her state senator, Jimmy Jawbus. The senator was not concerned, but he did take issue with accepting a bum rap.

Benito Bordosko, who lived in the middle of the city, was able to enjoy sleeping late on Saturday mornings because the skyscraper next to his apartment building blocked out the bright morning sunlight. The building was knocked down in the middle of the summer. He arose a little earlier than usual the next Saturday morning and told his mother that he was now unable to sleep, for all of the raze.

Lauren Latent had done renovations in her dining room that included decorating the edges and corners of the walls. On her two-week vacation, some water had leaked in through the window and left green residue on the walls. When Lauren returned from the beach, she invited several of her friends inside. Her best friend Marcy told her that she liked the renovations but was not a big fan of the molding.

Movie director Marvin Moller was trying to figure out which of his two actresses would best fit the parts of the leading ladies. One of the women, Cicely, a known diva, insisted on playing the role of Katherine. After several weeks of putting up with her and desiring to try Molly out in that role, Marvin decided that he did not want to "play Kate" Cicely any longer.

In the desert, a group of tourists noticed that there was a fossil-like structure of bee nests set against a canyon in a perfect semicircle. Surely, this must have been an arc hive.

A phenomenally attractive woman, Tamara Tepida, caught the eye of an eccentric fellow, Davey Delton. It was clear by Davey's behavior that he had not been on a date in a long time. When he asked Tamara out to dinner, she told him that she might have considered it had he not acted so disparate.

The two finalists in a playwriting contest seemed to be neck and neck; both mocked the government. One of the judges mentioned that he thought both plays were approaching parity.

The residents of Spanish Harlem decided to have a weeklong culture fest, commencing with a pork-cooking contest. Everyone cheered as it was announced that Alberto had taken first prize in the Carne Val.

Baseball coach Don Dieper went out with a car salesman to test-drive a new sports car. The salesman told him that the car was so dynamically balanced that it could exceed one hundred miles an hour without deviating from its center. Don ended up buying the car on the spot after they returned to the lot. He was a big fan of the line drive.

Dayton Drimmer, a known drunkard, used to imbibe and then roll around in the thick grasses behind his house. His family and friends tried to help bring him back to reality, but he would always respond that he enjoyed the lush life.

As an exhibition, the promoter of a dragster series would hire a group of women, wearing scant clothing, to compete. One mother stated that she was not going to let her teenage son attend the event since the entire spectacle was too racy.

Yvonne would take her nieces, Karen and Frances, to the mall to shop. While the girls were used to receiving differing amounts from their parents due to their ages, Yvonne was sure to give them each twenty dollars. Karen, years later, reflected back on these outings and realized that this method of allowance distribution was aunt equated.

Jermaine Jukus was super meticulous in the preparation of his saxophone prior to band practice, to the point where his fellow musicians thought he was OCD. He always seemed to miss out on warm-ups until finally the director questioned his reediness.

In an attempt to play off of the success of their ratings during the mid- and late nineties, a television network created a lineup of shows for Thursday evening's primetime schedule they thought would attract a huge audience. The first show in the time slot was a series based on the movie *Bambi*. The executives decided to call the evening "musk-see TV."

Grace Gerrands ran a bed and breakfast, and she usually had a couple of her nieces and nephews help her out in the summer. She instructed them that the customer is always right and that it was unwise to cross hostile boarders.

Grumpy old man Maxwell Maddux did not like his neighbor's rambunctious children, as they would often wander into his yard. He decided he would plant a row of prickly plants between the two homes to create an insurmountable burrier.

Three cowboys were trying to pick up women at a local saloon. Each man bragged about the quality of his boots. As the third cowboy, Terry, was talking about his, at the last second he took his boots off and held them up for everyone to see. His decision was very much spur-of-the-moment.

Kelly Koatail attended a parade in Thailand, where the spectators were encouraged to dress up in costumes. She wondered if she should be outlandish and dress up as a vault or just attend in more traditional garb. Her travel buddy, Deana Doldrum, told her that in this case it was better to be a safe than sari.

A pair of Siamese twins went looking for an apartment. Landlords would marvel at them but were cautious because of the laws concerning joint tenants.

The leaders of two countries that had been fighting for centuries decided to come together to discuss a peace treaty. After being excluded from a couple of closed-door meetings, the press wanted some information. One of the presidents told the journalists that while they were working on an agreement, the lingering conflict made the leaders not want to be too pacific.

A group of travelers was walking in a desert and encountered tradesmen with cargo, toting their animals. One traveler saw a llama-like animal with a certain luminescence about it. To the bewilderment of his peers, this man immediately ran in the opposite direction, exclaiming that he was repulsed by camel lights.

Melinda Masooni, a camp counselor, was in charge of a group of kids for the program's field day. Her group was given crimson as a team color, and they would wear shirts of that color in the competition. As they donned their uniforms, she was told that a few of the children had left their tops at home. Upset and anxious, she told them that they were going out to start the competition in five minutes, ruddy or not.

Father Melvin, one member on a team of priests at a large church, was looking to lead his own flock. He approached the archbishop with his proposal, and he was told to parish the thought.

A mother lion, Leona, watched her off spring, Lester and Louie, play together in the jungle. You could tell by her expression that the young cubs were her pride and joy.

A large group of fish got together to form a bop ensemble. The critics recognized them as part of the new school of jazz.

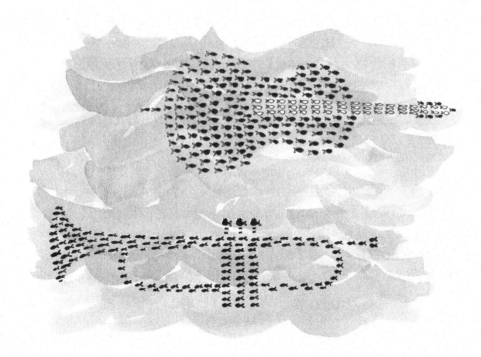

The baseball manufacturing plant created a new process for stitching, but it malfunctioned. Several of the defective balls slipped out onto the market. It was a darn shame.

Cain's brother's son was out in the woods, trying to chop some wood but being unsuccessful. His uncle encouraged him, saying he was born to be an Abel-bodied young man.

The football coach placed his men in a line to test their strength on the weight bench. Upon close examination, it seemed as if they were lined up from smallest to largest, based on chest size. It was as if the coach had created some sort of pecking order.

Allison Ashtree was once in an art gallery and ventured to a section featuring wildlife paintings. There was one painting that appeared to depict sheep grazing. Upon closer inspection, she noticed the animals' horns and verified that they were nothing more than a bunch of scapegoats.

Donna's eighty-seven-year-old grandfather, Ulysses Umber, accompanied the family on their summer vacation. He had been quite the grouch for the entire trip. In an effort to reconcile, he offered to pay for the next tank of gas for their SUV. Donna refused and told him that she was not a fan of fossil fuel.

Jackson Journier bought a band for his right hand to denote the birth year of each of his children, Stuart, Marion, and Tammy. These bands were very gaudy, and every time he held up his hand, it looked like a three-ring circas.

A group of young travelers scoured Europe. After several days on their trek, the young people were provided housing at a supervised bed and breakfast. They were encouraged to bathe, but Frankie Farrow resisted. His dad told him that when he was abroad, he should be wary of hostel waters.

During the holiday season, the Lowery family typically played a football game featuring the male cousins. Kevin and Sammy, the two oldest, were the captains. In two consecutive games, Sammy's team outscored Kevin's team handily. As soon as the game was over, the family dined. It was a Thanksgiving dinner with all the trimmings.

Monique Mayhigh loved visiting her Aunt Lula in the summertime. There were a couple of trees betwixt which a hammock was tied. The trees had beautiful copper leaves and sweet nuts to snack on. For Monique, even though she was inland, she enjoyed her days visiting the beeches.

In a bizarre occurrence, a woman in Australia gave birth to three cats. The head ob-gyn at the hospital was informed immediately and responded, "You have got to be kitten me."

A team of artists was commissioned to paint the side of a youth center downtown. The most experienced artist took on the lead role and decided that one quadrant of the wall would depict the torso of a Dalmatian. Some of the younger workers got out of hand with their horseplay and slacked off. After attempting to get them to go back on track and redo the spots, the leader finally yelled at them, saying, "All I want is a little re-speck!"

Ivan Irie, a pitcher known throughout the league for his arsenal of breaking balls, vomited on the mound nearly every outing, just prior to his first pitch. He thus became known as one of the nastiest hurlers in the league.

As a teen, Maria Marmalady visited France with her family every summer. Now that she had teens, she decided it would be a great time to return. Prior to their trip, she mentioned to her children that they would stay in a large, old mansion in the countryside. Her daughter asked whether the structure would remain intact. Maria responded, "Without a chateau of a doubt."

An attractive young woman caught the eye of Arthur Axewell, a popular acupuncturist around town. After about an hour of conversation, he asked her to go on a date with him the following Wednesday. However, she had many suitors and did not want to get pinned down with any commitments.

An artist was commissioned to paint a picture of Princess Pertrude, a striking woman with many strong features. The photo focused on her profile and really highlighted her pronounced nose. The photo was on display at a national gallery, and one of the viewers commented that he was not impressed by this poor trait.

Norwegian ice-park proprietor Perkan Pilgin told the press that he had captured the largest sea monster in history and that he would unveil it to the public the following Saturday at noon. Thousands lined up that weekend, anxiously awaiting arrival of the monster. After a half hour, one of the impatient newsmen yelled, "When are you going to go ahead and get things kraken?"

Irvin Ironday, a regionally recognized strong man, was asked to be a pallbearer at his great uncle's funeral. He commented that though he would volunteer, he had never been great at dead lifts.

Sanjay Sacrimone, a chubby teen, went to visit his auntie in the United Kingdom one summer. After his arrival, he immediately had his US money converted. After a few reckless spending sprees, Sanjay called his mother to give her an update. She was mistakenly ecstatic when he told her that he had lost more than a few pounds while visiting.

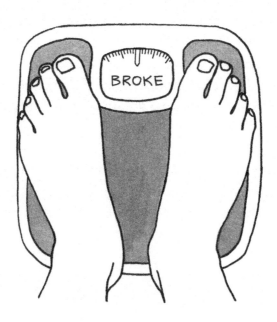

Diana Daytreat entered a coffee shop to join some of her friends for a bit of conversation. She caught the end of a topic about some countries that had agreed to stop their war. She asked whether or not that battle was currently happening stateside, but they told her it was over cease.

Herman Helflove wore a wonderfully smooth jacket that everyone noticed when he went out on the town. A stranger commented how nice it was, and Herman told him that it was made of goatskin. The man told him that he must be kidding.

Bjorn went to visit his cousin, Adrian, one afternoon to play some computer games. He noticed that Adrian's mother was in bed with some sort of illness and asked Adrian if she was infected with some sort of auntie virus.

A group of Nordic explorers started a trek. They decided they would stop somewhere between Russia and Sweden. Matthias Mastronje was an extreme type A, and he always nagged the captain as to when they would encounter the Finnish.

Martin Mandable would often use medicated rub to ease the pain in his bum shoulder at night. He had taken the bottle with him for a camping trip out in the woods and had only a little left with a few more days remaining on the trip. He wisely decided to salve it for later.

Cornelius Corbuss, a devout man, rented a boat to get across the river and achieve a higher level of spirituality on a deserted island a few miles away. As he was attempting to row away, he realized that he was getting nowhere. The boat owner asked from the top of the deck, "You've released the anchorite?"

Two young percussionists in a marching band would always clash their instruments on the wrong beat. The director noticed and announced to the rest of the ensemble that while great minds think alike, cymbal ones do as well.

Elton Etonight traveled to an amusement park with a medieval theme. He was getting into the knight's armor, and though he acknowledged to the park attendant that he'd never jousted before, he was willing to take a stab at it!

Angelo Arborjake, the head groundskeeper for a professional football team, told his oldest son, Bruno, that he needed him to help the crew repair the turf on the field that weekend. Bruno had to work instead of going on a date with Heather, the hottest girl in school; needless to say, this new reality soddened him.

In the last scene of the play, the mechanic saw the villain and brought him to his demise by repeatedly striking him in the stomach with his tool. Critics loved the ending and nominated it as one of the most gut-wrenching performances of the year.

DJ Les Son was a pioneer in hip-hop. He developed music that taught youth morals and offered guidelines on how to live their lives. Brian told his mom about the musician, but she was cautious; she wanted no part in her son listening to suggestive lyrics.

Chip Chaseround's high school coach was aware that although Chip was one of the fastest players on the team and should run tailback, Chip really wanted to follow in his father's footsteps and play safety. Coach Warner told Chip to think about his decision over the weekend. "As of right now, Coach," he said, "I'm leaning on de fense."

Elroy Ellersworthy used a prepaid mobile to impersonate others when making prank calls. Ultimately, he was subpoenaed for engaging in telephony.

As a matter of tradition, one of the Aboriginal tribes would present all of the young men entering adulthood as a group to the rest of the clan. Their faces were painted in warrior stripes, and they were given the hunting stick that they used to hunt animals from long distances. This was a very serious ceremony with spear ritual ramifications.

Enos Erieloe, a zany young comedian, was hired by a coffee company to appear in a series of catchy commercials. In one of them, he peeked over a countertop and stared at a hot cup of joe while making peculiar faces. After viewing the footage, the directors decided to bring him back in for another mugging the next day.

Lucien Leftander, the director of an independent film about angels, hired actors to play demons in the movie. He then rethought his decision and decided it would be wise to cast out devils.

After a daylong excursion on a party cruise, the participants were given a choice of hotels where they could choose to sleep the night. Sandra Stayon, not wanting to leave, mentioned that her preference was to stay at the merry yacht.

Stacey Sticker purchased some secondhand golf clubs over the Internet. She called the owner to inquire about them, and he told her that they were worth at least six hundred dollars because of their special handles, but he would sell them to her for only three hundred dollars. Excited, she took them to her cousin, a golf pro, for inspection. He told her that she had really gotten the shaft this time!

Yvonne Eversoll was visiting a remote island where they used many different forms of currency. In one case, she saw a woman pay for a piece of jewelry with what appeared to be a chicken breast, and Yvonne told her companion that she had never seen tender like that before.

Farrah Fairfeed bought her sweetheart, a bartender, a custom-made spigot for the kegs from which he poured beer. He really appreciated his love tap.

A group of five-star generals gathered at a remote location to discuss military strategy. Unfortunately, many of the men were sprayed by skunks on the way back to their cabins. General Lofton, the least senior of the group, was a little anxious, as he had never been around such a large group of rank officials.

Nisha Niceways, a huge fan of Bugs Bunny, loved to play her CD of music from the animated TV show on road trips. When she noticed Adam was annoyed, she asked him if he disliked her CD. He responded that he was just not a big fan of car tunes in general.

Riley Raysun and some of his friends were on a road trip to the beach. Riley had severe acid reflux, and on this trip he had an attack that was so intense he needed medical attention. Needless to say, his gastrointestinal problems really put a hiccup in the group's plans.

On his trip to Argentina, Bo Borso noticed that certain craftsmen were extracting oil from birds that appeared to be ostriches. After doing some research, Bo noticed that this oil was used for a special carpenter's glue. He wondered if this glue was nothing more than a paste rhea.

Fannie Farmous had been through many bad relationships with men. She found new love riding her filly mare, Lucky 8. She would go to visit her horse every day, as it was the first stable relationship she had had in many years!

Jackie Jakerun claimed to have the strongest toes in the world. One summer he decided to get a sports-supplement company to sponsor him on a tour of the country promoting this ability. When he visited his hometown, one of the acts involved him lifting a chain with a hundred-pound weight about eighteen inches off the ground. One observer admitted that this was one of the most impressive feets of strength she had ever seen!

Dwight Dudate was about to catch the train and noticed an interesting part on the grill that resembled a diamond stud. He was standing next to the ticketing agent and inquired about the piece. The worker told him that he didn't know anything about engine earring.

Quinn Questwater was quite a surfer. Over the years, he developed a following and used his platform to relay his militant political views to his fans. Many of the younger generation loved his extreme contemporary philosophy, and they thought he was, like, totally radical.

Poindexter Peteroff made it his mission to collect all of the program installation CDs that he loaned out during the semester. As the months passed, he retrieved them all. He told a bunch of his friends that in celebration, he was going to host a disk owe party.

Ola Mae Jenkins won a national award in a best grandmother contest. As part of the award, the committee had a live marching band play one of her favorite tunes. The committee noticed that she enjoyed it so much that they requested the band play it again as sort of a re-prize.

Clarence Capers went to an estate auction and picked up a vintage publicity shot of Clark Gable from the mid-twentieth century for only a hundred dollars. He showed the picture to his friend Lucien, a movie buff, and was told that the photograph was quite a still!

As a joke, young Simon Sezno would write, incorrectly, the location of the family home on the back of his father's shirt when he was napping. Once his dad found out, he gave Simon a lecture; the youngster needed to know how to properly address his elders.

CPSIA information can be obtained
at www.ICGtesting.com
Printed in the USA
BVOW06s0825111216
470410BV00036BA/990/P